THE THAMES
A PHOTOGRAPHIC MEANDER
by
Richmond & Twickenham Photographic Society

Foreword
by Sir Christopher Leaver, GBE

I live by the River and work by the River; and in the near future I shall be able to travel to work on the River Thames. More of that later.

As Deputy Chairman of Thames Water Authority and Chairman of the London Tourist Board, I am closely involved in promoting the use of the River Thames. For many years I have longed to see life and activity on this great highway of our capital.

Therefore it gives me much pleasure to introduce this selection of photographs taken on and near the River Thames by members of the Richmond and Twickenham Photographic Society. They represent but a fraction of the 350 or so photographs which form part of the exhibition entitled "Project Thames" which was first shown at the Orleans House Gallery, Twickenham, for three months from June 1987 and then toured many other galleries along the Thames.

The Richmond and Twickenham Photographic Society has been established for nearly 100 years (anniversary in 1990) and its membership of almost 300 were delighted to be asked by the much younger River Thames Society, celebrating its 25th anniversary, to produce an exhibition on the theme of the River. 3,000 photographs were sent in by eager members and after much soul-searching 350 have been chosen, some of which are seen in this booklet.

The Thames from Southend to Lechlade and beyond is covered in its many moods and seasons. Starting from Southend the voyage takes us, by sailing barge even, through the spectacular Thames Barrier, opened by the Queen in 1982 and on to that symbol of London – Tower Bridge. As Lord Mayor of London in 1982 I was thrilled to have had the honour to open officially the Walkway and Tower Bridge Museum to visitors. The walkways were always intended to be used by pedestrians. When the Bridge was first opened in 1904 the traffic along the River was heavy and the Bridge was constantly opened to ships. But the walkways proved a haven for unsavoury characters and were soon closed.

Today they provide a unique viewing platform, especially for photographs, not only of the River but of the City and docklands. The museum shows the beam engines which once lifted the roadway. And, yes, a bus was once caught hanging on by its rear wheels as the Bridge opened.

The River from here to Westminster is well-known and well-loved – thousands of tourists travel by sightseeing boat to enjoy the panorama of buildings and the full appreciation of the historic bridges under which they pass.

Once past the Houses of Parliament – a building designed to be enjoyed at its best from the River – the river banks are less well-known, although up-river boat services operate through the summer.

Battersea Power Station is just one of several massive relics of another era that still survive on our river banks. It is hard to reconcile the outcry from conservationists who wanted it preserved when it closed as a power station ten years ago with the horror that greeted its first appearance in the '30s when Londoners saw it as "a monstrosity, a blot on the landscape and a source of pollution". Well, the source of pollution is gone; London's air now only suffers from traffic fumes, but the building remains and is being turned into a fantasy world – an indoor and outdoor leisure park for Londoners and visitors.

Further along the Thames, new developments are joining the old, such as the picturesque Strand on the Green, to provide attractive housing with enviable river views.

Kew Gardens and Richmond Hill in the snow convey a completely different atmosphere of two places Londoners have come to love. And further on is Hampton Court Palace, on most visitors' itinerary, and a treasure-house of paintings. We don't see them here, but I welcome the fact that the avenue of lime trees which once adorned the Great Fountain Court has been replanted – all 198 of them, 20ft high.

A beautiful shot of herons remind us here of the natural wildlife which thrives in and around the River Thames. Further along we see the swans at Windsor. Her Majesty the Queeen and the Dyers' and Vintners' livery companies are still the only people entitled to own swans on the River Thames.

A sweep past Henley reminds me that it now also stages a most successful arts and music festival hot on the heels of its famous regatta; and so we reach Oxford, Newbridge and Lechlade. Delightful stopping points for those who take a cruising holiday along this stretch of the River Thames. We end peacefully with a meadow in contrast to the bustling estuary at Southend.

I am now taking my involvement with the River further with a company called Thames Line plc. We have launched a commuter service which we hope will grow and become established – not only so that many may travel to and from their offices – but for the millions of Londoners like me who wish to see the River return to its prominence as London's major artery.

Ten years from now I would hope that another exhibition on this subject would show gleaming new piers, attractive riverside walkways, more pubs, restaurants and cafeterias overlooking the River, and above all, more traffic up and down the mighty Thames.

Sir Christopher Leaver, GBE

Cocklers Boat in Winter, Leigh-on-Sea
Jane Miller

Southend Pier
Jane Miller

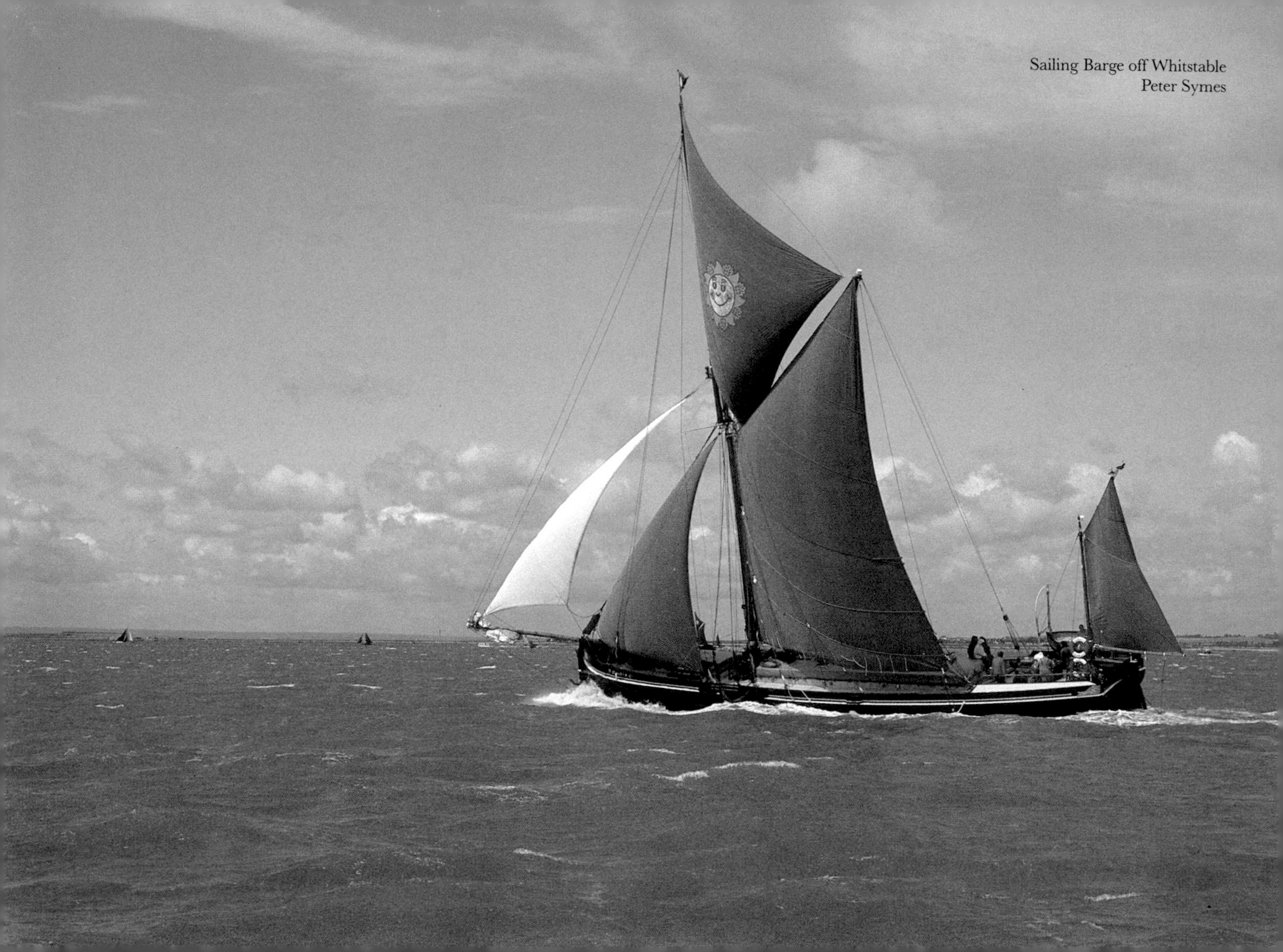
Sailing Barge off Whitstable
Peter Symes

Bait-Diggers, Southend on Sea
Jane Miller

Thames Barrier – Testing
Terry Hollands

King George V Dock
Derek White

Reflections – St Katherine's Dock
Tony Marshall

St Katherine's Dock
Derek White

Southwark Bridge
Peter Symes

Paul's and the City
ter Symes

King's Reach
Peter Symes

Westminster Bridge
Peter Symes

Houses of Parliament and
Westminster Abbey
Derek White

Westminster Bridge at night
Alan Richards

Battersea Power Station
Peter Symes

Founder's Day – Chelsea Hospital
Jane Miller

Putney Embankment
Jane Miller

EMBANKMENT SW15

3T
Except
Buses

HAMMERSMITH
BRIDGE

Hammersmith Bridge
John Barnett

High Tide, Strand on the Green
Jane Miller

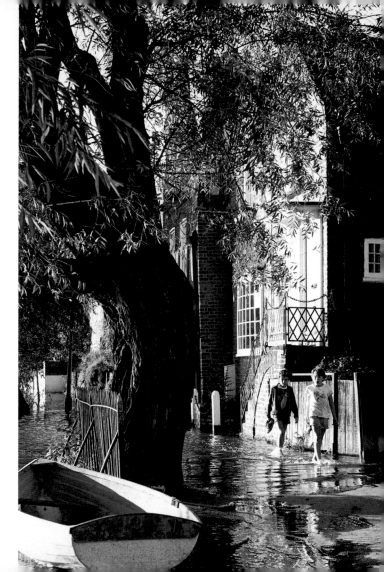

Kew Bridge
Andrew Chapman

Brentford Lock 1st on Thames
Jane Miller

Kew Gardens, Winter
Jane Miller

Kew Gardens in snow storm   Jane Miller

Syon House   Jay Charnock

View from Richmond Hill – Winter   Lucilla Phelps

Orleans House Gallery, Twickenham   George Morris

Hampton Court –Winter
Martin Western

Hampton Court Bridge
Mary Bennet

Shepperton Lock   George Morris

Chertsey Bridge   George Morris

Staines Town Hall   George Morris

Bell Weir Lock   George Morris

Paddle steamer, Runnymede   H. S. Fry

Windsor Castle across river   Jane Miller

Changing guard Windsor Castle   Alex Luke

Long Walk, Windsor   George Morris

Morning Ride, Datchet, near Windsor   Jane Miller

Marlow Jane Miller

River in flood, Marlow
Jane Miller

Hambleden Mill
Jane Miller

Oxford Poly's Eight, Henley
Lucilla Phelps

Cambridge Blue in skiff, Henley   Lucilla Phelps

Henley out of Season   Jane Miller

Clifton Hampden Bridge   H. S. Fry

Four Spot Chaser Dragon-fly   Ray Winslade

Radcliffe Camera, Oxford
Lucilla Phelps

Rowing Eight, Oxford
John Barnett

Brasenose College Sundial, Oxford   John Barnett

Newbridge Reflection   Betty Barnes

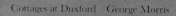
Cottages at Duxford   George Morris

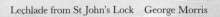
Lechlade from St John's Lock   George Morris

Lechlade Rowing Boats   Tony Marshall

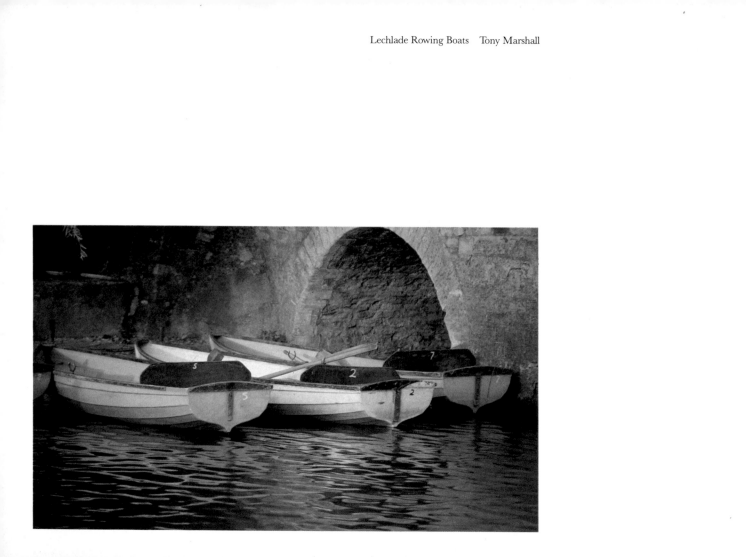

Lechlade Boat Yard   George Morris

Upstream from Ha'penny Bridge, Lechlade   George Morris